SAID THROUGH GLASS

Said Through Glass

Poems

JONA COLSON

2018 Jean Feldman Poetry Prize Winner

Washington Writers' Publishing House
Washington, D.C.

COVER PHOTO by SHTTEFAN on Unsplash
COVER DESIGN by Meg Reid
BOOK DESIGN by Barbara Shaw

Library of Congress Cataloging-in-Publication Data

Names: Colson, Jona, 1979- author.
Title: Said through glass : poems / Jona Colson.
Description: Washington, DC : Washington Writers' Publishing House, [2018]
Identifiers: LCCN 2018030233 | ISBN 9781941551189 (pbk.)
Classification: LCC PS3603.O466 A6 2018 | DDC 811/.6—dc23
LC record available at https://lccn.loc.gov/2018030233

Printed in the United States of America

WASHINGTON WRITERS' PUBLISHING HOUSE
P. O. Box 15271
Washington, DC 20003

ACKNOWLEDGMENTS

My thanks to the magazines and anthologies where some of these poems first appeared (often in earlier forms):

Antioch Review: "Job Interview"
Barrelhouse: "The Other Life"
Beloit Poetry Journal: "Las Meninas II (Maribárbola) and "Las Meninas V (Nicolas Pertusato)"
Broad River Review: "Prayer"
Crab Orchard Review: "Retina"
Flyway: A Literary Journal: "Jonah's Whale"
FOLIO: "Havana" and "Tulips"
Harpur Palate: "My Mother's Hands" and "A Sea So Quiet"
Lake Effect: "Among Panicles of Spent Flowers"
Little Patuxent Review: "The Orange Speaks"
Painted Bride Quarterly: "Mother, Rest"
Palooka: "God-help and Sparrow"
Ploughshares: "The Last Time I Saw My Father"
Prairie Schooner: "Grief" and "Self"
Subtropics: "Doctor to Patient"
The Florida Review: "Dive" and "Happy as a Clam"
The Massachusetts Review: "House for Sale" (published as "At the Open House")
The Potomac Review: "Doctor to Patient (II)"
The Southern Review: "Passport Control"
The Southampton Review: "Snow"
Stoneboat Literary Journal: "A Year after My Father Died"
Zone 3: "When a Bee is Caught"

"From the Wrist and Reaches" and "My Father's Dream" first appeared in *Flicker and Spark* (Lowbrow Press) edited by Regie Cabico and Brittany Fonte.

"St. Valentine Speaks" and "Doctor to Patient (III)" were first published in *Stoked Words* (Capturing Fire Press) edited by Regie Cabico.

CONTENTS

I

PASSPORT CONTROL

What brings you to this country?

My mother once told me that my breath is strong enough to diamond a grain of sand.

What is the nature of your visit?

After the plane took off, I felt gravity surrender. There is no safety.

How long will you be here?

It depends on what you consider love? It could be days, or something brief said through glass.

What are your plans?

The cabin steamed as we passed the equator. All my plans got wet, and I was showered with a warm mist.

What hotel are you staying in?

Another room is the same as the first. If I close my eyes, I am back in my boyhood bedroom, years collapsing under my feet.

Will you be traveling outside the country?

I learn borders like some men learn kitchens—blundering through the knife-edged drawers and slicing my fingers like cherries. I tend to leave stains.

Have a good stay.

My body is awake. There are birds that only follow rivers. They alight on small rocks and feed on the wing in the morning sunglare.

DIVE

To step beyond the ledge, arch
and fall into water.

To be worth your weight
you need to take your last breath

as if it were your last
so you cut the surface and leave

no bruise. Align your fingers,
your arms, your elbows

and curve your body for break.
At any temperature the depth

may begin to feel warm and soft,
and you may mistake this for love until

you try to breathe.

DOCTOR TO PATIENT

What brings you here today?

A pain, it runs down my arm during the night.

When did it start?

A few years ago when I saw a bee land on a mint leaf.

How does the pain feel?

When it snows, like electricity.

Are you taking anything for it?

I read a story about a woman who vanished, maybe she just turned herself into a fish.

May I examine your arm?

Touch is strange. I wonder if fish feel it when you slice their bellies.

Does this hurt?

There is no rule that states I must remain human.

Can you bend your arm?

When I was five, I broke this arm because it wanted attention. I think it still does.

Does it hurt only at night?

Yes, I dream I am a thin man, slicing down tobacco leaves—large like green oars.

Let me check your blood pressure.

My heart is beating in sixteenth notes.

I'm going to listen to your heart.

I've never seen the heart of a fish. They don't sell that at the market.

Everything is fine, is there anything else?

I feel like a man with the rope around his neck.

MY MOTHER'S HANDS

A tapestry of silk once stretched tight now hangs loose
and yields with creases and paths. The skin on her hands
is almost nothing, yet I know she held me,

malleable and male, in a yellow bolt
of cloth—her fingernails trimmed back as far as
possible to avoid scratching newborn skin.

Now, her fingers turn and twist against themselves,
like stems of wild roses—reaching out
into delicate air. When she holds me at the door,

I know her hands understand the cool love
to fever, the light to heat, and chests of days
that close around us, and I can sometimes

feel her fingers straighten and her skin tense
vowing to hold strong and smooth as if years
collapsed and the nerves refused to age.

GOD-HELP AND SPARROW

Cloaked in skin and muscle, it protrudes
like an orange—and while her neck is hyper-extended, arching away
from an electric sun as if she were a strange branch weighted with nests at its tips,

the nurse pierces it with the fine needle as my mother prays
for roots against the white parchment of the surgical table
and for neighbors of apple and pear, and calls

God-help and sparrow while she imagines it fluttering, as if she had
swallowed a butterfly with only one wing growing, but the fluid comes out

against its desire and the nurse, looking satisfied, holds the vial,
like a potion, up to the light, saying, *yes, yes, yes.*

WHEN A BEE IS CAUGHT

This is mother and wood—both rooted in blossom.
My grandmother's dust not far away.

They can't catch these threads of web rippling
through the air like wings.

When a bee is caught, he panics in the soft strands, but I wind
my patience around it—no struggle—only

harmony and gold
in my tune, and like him

I'm left alone, veined to flowers
pulling out silk from my mouth.

DOCTOR TO PATIENT (II)

Do you celebrate love?

I am unable to say. I never look it in the eye.

Even though you know what it does?

Slice the underbelly and peel it back. Flesh always heals faster.

Is there a plan?

Only the path of jealousy. The city I need to learn, the eagerness to know roads, names, and photographs.

What if it fails?

I observe. I think of white oleander, lilacs, and irises. I will always feel this tremor in my thighs.

Are you nervous?

Last night I dreamed of rabid dogs. They ran up to the fence against my face, clawing and famished.

Why rabid dogs?

I rely heavily on memory, hair, fibers, and the feeling of a torn fingernail trail against a taut stomach.

Which means?

Hours go by, and I only need my imagination's rendering of the past.

Is that the truth?

It is not invention, but I have become braver. I see plumage sparking with stars before I begin to fly. The sky is soaked with light.

Is there always light?

I prefer to be in between. I never look it in the eye.

RETINA

No sudden darkness, no curse, but a slow black
curtain falling over the eye, almost like being born
again, my mother said.
                    And the next day: surgery,
to fasten the retina, like wallpaper, back to the frazzled
optic nerve and satisfy its hunger for impulse
and clear astonishment of light.

                    When I saw her after,
I felt like I was catching the sun in an intimate moment.
Still drowsy from halothane and smelling like blood, she slid off
the hospital bed toward the bleached bathroom. The bruised eye
beginning to focus the first wave of vision with the bandage removed,
the angry slivers aligning to exert her restored sight to the raw unmediated glare
while I held fast to her and we both stared
until it hurt.

MORNING TALK

How did you sleep?

I shuttered like the naked branches in the gusts.

Was your room too hot?

As if I were doused with thimblefuls of red lava.

Your eyes look red?

I was only soothed when the bone-colored moon emptied into my eyes.

Would you like some coffee?

The room smelled like the crisp air of snow just falling.

Toast? Tea?

I waited for the spinning solid hot globe beneath it.

Any plans for today?

A voice floating through channels in my brain.

I hope you had enough sleep.

I was suddenly caught between the dark and the light. I live sweeping past small stars.

TULIPS

Thrusting the white strangled hearts
into the musk and amber of October

graves, I heard them scream words
like fire and water, overwhelmed by

the smell of turned earth and stone,
they are not close enough, over millions,

over the world's chaos, their colors rolling out
only to end with green pushing down

like desperate nails. So strange the autumn,
exposing death, clean as an almond shelling itself.

THE WEDDING PHOTOGRAPH

After 47 years you climb the stairs,
call his name, and no one answers.

You see him in his room
huddled in a blue sheet
call out his name

and no one answers.
You bend over his face
as a mother to a child

and suddenly life without
blazes around you
like a rare new planet

exploding from the window.

SELF

What am I made of? Eggs over easy
and white toast. A mid-April notion

of love under spring's harsh blossom,
or a basket of red coxcombs and daisies

beside my father's casket.
It's hard to think beyond the house

on the hill—the garden filled with
corn and radishes. When I was five,

I slept by a watermelon in the full moon
and woke up to walk in the grasslands

that are now covered in new homes and fences.
Perhaps I am merely anxious puffs of breath at 3 a.m.

since my mother said I am cursed and belong
elsewhere only to be missed someday.

GRIEF

After my father died
my sister started

looking for signs:
a slanted picture frame,

a bird by the window,
a sudden breeze.

Everything meant something.
The world offered

chocolate cake, homemade
breads, and vases of white lilies.

Inside, with mirrors knocked over
and dishes piling in the sink,

we accepted condolences
and smiled, while each

outside touch
burned brighter than grief.

LESSON

It wasn't until a few years
before he died when I came

down the stairs on a Saturday
morning and saw my father

by the kitchen window,
shirtless, ironing fresh

blue tea towels,
that I understood why

my mother fell in love.

FROM THE WRIST AND REACHES

It is hard to remember him,
but I can see my father in his quiet August:

a young man, handsome and blue-eyed,
his smile not yet crooked and small.

I see him in the garden picking tomatoes
from their strangled green vines—

the time of year that opens from the wrist and reaches—

he smells of summer and dirt. Hot and alive,
a wire in my throat.

MY FATHER'S DREAM

My father wanted me to
wrestle alligators in
central Florida
and eat fresh rattlesnake
down in San Antonio.

But I slept through
my father's dream
and woke up holding
a bundle of yellow tulips
that looked like the

early afternoon sun
of New York City.

II

HOUSE FOR SALE

Thank you for coming to the open house.

Outside I saw the flagstones moving like heads in a Picasso painting—black beetles for eyes.

The house was built in 1885.

The space unpeopled yet so alive. The sky torn off but still dusted with clouds.

There are three bedrooms and two full baths.

My father died in his bed, silent and cooling like the steel kettle my mother used for tea.

There is a new heating and cooling system.

I can't translate summers and winters into another language.

You have views of downtown.

I sometimes see my life as a wolf—galloping toward an open window, listening to the moon move.

Only a ten-minute walk to the metro.

The moon makes a soft hissing sound. You can hear through the doors. No way out or in. The day will come when my feet leave this floor. Take them with softness in your hands.

Feel free to make an offer.

When I was five, I ran through a glass door. It cut me before I had a chance to cry.

The owners are willing to negotiate.

I feel like an oyster building a pearl around a grain of sand. There are some truths I don't own.

HONEY

It pours from a jar, amber and combed
too thick to understand.

It softens the parched skin
rubbed in small fingerfuls.

It soothes the throat
when we stir it into tea.

At breakfast, it sweetens the morning toast
while we talk of summer—

hopeful as a bee toward a tulip
promising pollen.

HAVANA

What would make me stay?

Ripe plantains baked in rum
wrapped in green jaquiri leaves.

Dulce de fruta bomba from Santa Lucía,
carrying the stinging scent of sea fog.

Perhaps that unnamed species of orchid
we called *la Reina Sofía*.

Maybe a change of light—
a crescent moon floating white as a rib
at the edge of the sky.

That one red parrot to remind us
we are neighbors of fire

could keep me here
more than a few months—
come and go

hovering over sun-stained streets
and through sugarcane fields, a city
that almost hurts.

ST. VALENTINE SPEAKS

I started earlier when you had
no current or breath, and life

was pure hunger.
I can help you choose a ripe

apple, or teach you to pearl
milk on a June afternoon.

I am certain that everybody
has a heart, except some people

whose eyes blink in surprise
to touch or grace.

I will trouble your silence
with a sunset that pinks

the entire sky, and wake
you from a sleep where

your father's kiss was all
you knew of love.

CLEOPATRA'S HANDMAID

There was no snake—
no famed asp or cobra
coiling among
ripe, black figs.

Only the sound of glass
tingling in the sun
and her hand falling
slowly toward

the marble floor
where I waited
to be lionized.

THE WOMAN WHO BIT HER HUSBAND'S HAND

Next to me, the woman who bit her husband's hand—
her teeth sank into his flesh so hard
she speared bone. She tells me to smell
my own flesh—the taste and flavor
of one's skin—where I used to rub
my forehead when I sweated, where
I used to practice kissing, open-mouthed
so I could taste the salt. She stares
at my arm, reaches out to me, and tells me
to close my eyes.

REST CURE

Quite like the old times, the room says.
And I am here, with the narrow street outside,
what they call the impasse. They reach,

their hands pulling at the seams, guarded
locked, and hidden. This tender rim of steel
and wood, as if cure, as if undoing the gentle

folds of the fabric I clutch like a child against
this rest—stillness and the voice empty.

THE BEAUTIFUL DROWNED MAN

Black-matted hair
slippery flesh

I fished him from the sea
pulling him from warm water
easily and gently
like a blue scarf
from a pulsing neck

How beautiful he is

and how lost I had been
on a dark, cold night
before he stirred
and troubled
the pools of mud
around my feet.

THE ORANGE SPEAKS

For a moment, I forgot my fat, round self.
I forgot my fear of falling and the black

flies that siphon my pith and scent.
For a moment, I broke this fruitful

hook and circled the blossomed grove,
surveying human, spider, lizard, and snake.

For a moment, I clung to this slender
branch and remembered when I grew

among lavender and cinnamon—
I did not know what would become of me:

food for mosquitoes or perfumed oil.
For a moment, I savored the strange fingers

pulling me down and saw the canopy
of white bloom and green leaf above and knew

my place at the cusp of that waiting tongue.

SNOW

There is a promise in its lattice light,

its sway and spiral in white fury, falling

granular glint and glimmer, the way I'm brought

to the window following flakes in mid-flight.

There is a need to draw my name in its wet slate,

the terrible urge to disappear

into its folds, the slide and sunder of ice

and sphere, the hasty crush under heavy foot

as I raise it to my mouth—savor of sky,

of wood-fire, edged with anise and brume.

DOCTOR TO PATIENT (III)

Why does winter frighten you?

I'm afraid the air might snap into pieces.

Has that ever happened?

One winter when I was ten, I blew into the sky and the stars shattered.

How do you know?

Look, there is a half-moon scar next to my right eye.

I don't see it, perhaps an icicle fell?

No. It is as real as that knife in your hand.

I don't have a knife. This is a pen.

If you leave it open on the snow, she comes out—echoing in the chilled air.

Who comes out?

In the same breath, your bones quiver. Your belly shrouded in ice.

Does that mean you see someone?

One morning my mother asked me if I missed her when she was not there.

Is your mother alive?

I told her I missed her when I looked down at my cereal.

Do you mind if I write that down?

Knives are lonely—like a sliver of moon in a frozen sky.

III

LAS MENINAS

After the painting by Diego Velázquez

I. La Infanta Margarita

Hoop-skirt heavy, she waits in
yellow to be painted. Will he capture
her weight? Weight is what the hand
wants.

Weight is what the princess
possesses. The small yellow bulb
in the castle. Ten years later
she will tell a warrior, *te quiero*,
but he will die on a small Greek island.

Heart-heavy, she rises, oiled and
drowsy, surging on, with no anchor,
only a painting of her, here and there.
He never knew that

even after dusk, she still
shows yellow.

II. Maribárbola

After the painting, she plays hopscotch,
shy, sugar-colored legs vaulting in sudden sun.

The princess watches, her petite laughter
boring through Maribárbola's dreams like a dung beetle.

High up, in another world, clouds cluster and obstruct
sunlight—a *mariposa* rises from a fire-striped tulip,

dragoning down to the fall of an undersized foot,
Maribárbola topples over—shock of bruise—snap of bone,

the *mariposa* darts from the earth-twitch, only to tell
a berry finch how the little girl fell

and how the princess laughed.

III. Doña Marcela Ulloa

"She's always been a petty child."
Ever since her brother was pulled from the water's rim,
two days dead, during a hot day in Sevilla, Doña Marcela
has bowed to the pale rose called La Infanta Margarita.

"One day, I found her eating ants."
She circles the orbit of loss, trying not to think
of glossed ripples and swollen, white flesh. She had
no strength to untangle him from the weeds and brush.

"I do hope she doesn't catch fever."
Most days her body is too heavy, her arms cannot
clasp the buttons of the Queen's dress, her sleep-breathing
weighted with night-black waters of Sevilla.

IV. Doña María Agustina

I will love you no matter what atrocities
time commits.
             The first time I held
your hair because of the sudden wind
was the first time I remember anything.
This cup I offer you is clean, clean as bone,
clean as stone. Drink deep the water.

Look how they descend: the light,
the words—all things released
seek you.

The death itself—
an apt knife blade left
open on the field.

V. Nicolas Pertusato

The princess wants him, not Maribárbola,
in the room when she sleeps. She wants
to hear him laugh when the tame dog
licks his face like a soup spoon. She wants
to drift to sleep, pressing a knee or an elbow
into his back and sculpt her world, forgetting
her father's silence, the strict lessons, the pinch
on her left arm—bruising violet before she wakes.

VI. Don Diego Velázquez

Poised like stones in a river—
I capture their weight and movement, the sheath of light
from the open window, a glance of grace.
                              There are easier scenes:
a man drinking wine beside a lamp; a woman reading
a book under two trees; the relationship between figures
A and B.
                    But, I am amid beauty here.
Skin is felt and raised. The Queen's thoughts travel
around the room, her gaze pushing my brush like
wind. In the Royal Palace, she wants me to paint
drops of life, women rippling in nakedness longing
for a greater distance. She is mad to mourn alone:
A well gone dry with dust at the bottom.
                              The subject
shifts. I decide to use a variation of white—tempered
with saffron. Every point in space is crucial, the relationships
between the subject and the sound—a voice calling for water,
footsteps on the stair. I have been taught lines and perspective.
There is no brushstroke without color. Without the mirror,
I would not have been able to paint.

VII. Don José Nieto Velázquez

When the new candles were lighting
the dark sky of Madrid, lighting
so completely they were vanishing,
he put his face against the wall separating
him from the Queen, and heard
talk of empires, and the small princess,
and heirs wearing gold crowns. He heard
the Queen utter *no hijo, no hijo*, while
the other voice, soothed, became a song,
and he imagined the Queen's body
suddenly bending like soft wax.

VIII. La Reina Mariana

In Vienna, I lived close to the sky. Here,
everything arches away. My body is empty
and closed. When he touches me, I shiver
like a root in the rain.

                       I have a hundred
delays for a son, a male heir to rise up
from the soil and meet me, wrapped in
white lace and sprigs of thyme. The night
after Margarita was born, all I did was cry.
In Vienna, I lived close to the sky.

IX. El Rey Felipe IV

I am crushed. He sits in the dark and sees
how the light of the city fills the clouds.

He tries to remain hidden, framed with the Queen
in a mirror on the wall. He is interested in anger

and tries to find the source—he checks the rooms,
peering under huge furniture where he finds small

creatures—not quite cats not quite rats—licking
their narrow red jaws. *I am crushed.* Every night

he wakes to this anger—under the weight of his own
reflection. He tries to avoid the city, those who remind

him of his failures—lost empires and confused states.
I am crushed. He tries to listen for the click of the lock,

for the call from the one who pulls stars through a telescope,
for someone to tell him how to kiss softly a woman's eyes.

X. Doña Isabel de Velasco

waits for a summer morning

when there is no demand,
no need from the princess.

The slight lowering of the body,
the bending of knees

pleases and calms. After she
dresses her in the rustling gown

of pale satin, she returns
to her room and sees that her

own dress needs mending.

XI. Guardadamas

I don't think you understand. I am here
to protect her. And if I tried
something else, something
outside of myself, you would
know that the worst of me
is an accident of hope.

When she plays and laughs
I stand still as bone,
aware of everything around
her. I know the slightest breeze
in the branches, or the shift
of roots—and I pray
that her will is bright
enough to shadow
hope.

IV

JOB INTERVIEW

Thank you for coming. Did you have a hard time finding our office?

If I close my eyes, I can turn into a dove—star-crossed and searching in the sun.

Why are you interested in this position?

They say the man who invented the steam engine was inspired by watching a tea kettle.

Describe the best boss you've ever had.

Patience and happiness—like discovering a new species.

Best qualities?

I've been told that I blush easily in the afternoon.

Weaknesses?

There is something pith-edged and bitter about infidelity.

There are gaps in your resume.

It wasn't my intention to mislead you.

Why are you planning to leave your current position?

My mother taught me that meat is cooked when bone is removed easily from flesh.

What do you do in your spare time?

Kisses often fall and stain like pollen in a breeze.

Tell me one thing about yourself that is not on your resume.

I once looked into the heart of an artichoke—its core was thistle and stem.
No temptation and so far from its purple blossom.

What will you do if the position is not offered to you?

A cold bud shivers inside—not a breath or bee in sight.

If our roles were reversed, what questions would you ask?

Could we start again? I know now what requires a light touch.

HAPPY AS A CLAM

Happy I cannot see the gull's beak
      glide so close to the surface—

that beak that could shatter
      and smash me

helpless at the heart
      of my broken home.

Happy when the sweet
      tide rises and I bury myself

in sand where you will
      not find me. Happy

when the ocean calms me,
      its song a dark dreaming

of currents without hands or wings.

THE MAINSAIL

One hour out my body buckled
and the Chesapeake turned to a brackish
film reflecting a sun too hot for May

as the boat jolted starboard
with the calculated rise of the mainsail—
the taut fabric like a drumskin stretched
from water to sky—

such anxiety
while I wrung my hands from the lines:
a matter of tension and the intangible way
of holding things I'd just as soon let go.

A ROOM COOL AS PEARLS

is something I want
       to last forever.

A sun throwing dawn
       across the air,

the sounds of breathing
       through space like hair,

a body, familiar and satin,
       across thin blue sheets.

The way to hold is afterwards
       so clear, and perhaps

this is our time to amaze each other.

THE LAST TIME I SAW MY FATHER

The last time I saw my father
sound and marrow-filled,

he was standing on the front porch—
almost the weight

of a ghost. As I waved goodbye,
I felt a nerve twitch—

like a dog's ear batting a fly.
He never sold me the world.

He never said that people
are good. But the next morning

when he stopped like a hare
snapped in the steel trap,

my name knelt down
beside him and the smallest

sigh became a lullaby.
I touched his hand

and, like any good son,
straightened his dark hair

before they carried him
out into the air.

AMONG PANICLES OF SPENT FLOWERS

I believe the night will be too cluttered
with moths and ghosts to breathe,

or a loss will pierce me so deeply
I may keep asking for more.

PUSH THE HEART

All the pretty ones return to mother and ask for help,
or a head, or a hand, or a heart, if there are

some extra ones (not too expensive) they can have in the yard.
So, push the heart, mother, push it

like a barge inside the rib cage, push it till
the pulses sync with mine

and the ones who beg lose
their heads.

MOTHER, REST

I, too, felt anxious, and snared—
so when I left the house
I didn't wave goodbye,
didn't look you in the eye.
I knew I would not come back
to that room, that sound of stars
crashing against the window mesh,
that color of loss sword-flashing silver
in the dark hall. I couldn't take you

with me. I couldn't take all
those bruised scraps. Just try to rest, Mother,
rest against the fence. I'll hold
you here from outside.

PRAYER

They gathered around the table
like lambs bleating in the dark.

They hooked their hands in a circle
and waited for an answer or an ambiguous

reply from a child absent flesh and bone.
There were sudden sharp sighs when

a soft cry sounded far in the corner
and a breeze wafted onto the table.

Perhaps the hint of an instruction,
or the beginning of a belief,

or simply a surge of relief when,
in the end, there was no language

except in bellows.

LATIN

Here are *animal* and *aquatic*—creatures
hiding in their swollen beds.

There are a few ways to disappear: forget
the names of friends, be an apparition

or a ghost whose weight is in limbo.
Here are *history* and *atlas*—language, tongue,

and literal. How embarrassing to be so close
to failing in love and strung up by the ankles

until the truth falls out like *aviary* and *devour*—
a whole summer ushering out flies that ate pink at the bone.

MIDNIGHT AT THE BOAT DOCK

The boats rocking quietly in their dark slips
do not care that the heron

taught me how to catch a fish with my feet.
Or, how the slug rocked me slowly

into shallow water. They don't listen
when I ask them to watch me lie face up

in the water, even when the tide rushes in,
and I am calm against its thrash.

The water holds me, but the boats understand
and teach me to wait without waiting

and look to the sky relieved with stars
while a single spider spins its wet web

between the planks. They remember their voyages
and the deep privacy of the sea.

The safety of the moor and longing of the drift.
I hear how the water belongs to them,

and for a while it belongs to me.

A YEAR AFTER MY FATHER DIED

I dreamed
his death

an excursion.
I began walking

through a familiar
woods, like the one

behind our house.
I kept walking

and climbed over
a childhood fort—

made from a fallen
oak tree, carved

like a cave. I sloshed
through a stream—

ankle deep
in fresh water

boots agitating
small grey fish

that slipped
from my fingers.

Then,
it all stopped,

89

and I threw
down my backpack,
looked up, and said,
there you are.

THE STAIRS

My mother negotiates the steps
like rocks up a steep mountain
and bears on the wooden railing
so hard it creaks and its smooth

skin bends in worn intervals.
When she reaches the landing,
her lungs let out a release,
and she pauses to remember

her mother lifting her from a chair
when there was no weight,
and she became a leaf
delivered into the wind.

A SEA SO QUIET

You would think I go mad with grief
when the white sails fill—billowing out

like a pregnant belly into the cold sky
making no sound. It is a sea so quiet even the waves

are silenced in their swells. I am taught to interpret
these signs—the slight of the keel, the swing of the boom—

as we ghost past Thomas Point Lighthouse.
The keel cuts like a marble blade through the brackish water,

the stern refuses to wake, and the Captain, deciding
not to fight, learns to live here, though it is bitter

in his throat—the way silence affects everyone in the end.
But, even the sea a vow of dumbness? Nobody touches.

We are the only two in existence—all hands forward to strike
and secure the mainsail. Time ceases where invisible

figures move below the surface—how much life can be
kept in by the sea, how much clings to the surface of the boat,

a space where seaweed holds to fiber bathed by water.
I will stay here until the seaweed takes root and the fossils surface

because the quiet present dissolves like salt
and soon sound will drown us all out.

WRONG LOVE

Something pure-edged
and burning

when I see
the doorway
the rooms
the night
the world

and on the other side

somewhere

you laugh
you drink
you eat

and slam a car door,
driving down streets
un-alone

as my body forms
one arch of a cry.

JONAH'S WHALE

We sail out on the first weekend of the season
into a north-northwest wind
over a springing bay of fish and crab.

I rest on the stern, burning my mouth on a wind-hot ash
and watch the lighthouse pass by as easily as hands
navigate a new body. I think my mother will soon die.

What a strange thought to have sailing toward the bridge
under a hot sun—only two hours out and already there is death.
I think there is something beneath us, perhaps a whale. Only it is

not. We are in the bay, not the ocean where I can go days and weeks
and never reach land. I decide I am on the whale, its belly full of me,
full of Jonah, and the cockpit, two berths, two heads and galley.

Being inside I know this is how one starts a planet and keeps digging to forget
light and diesel fuel. Inside this whale, I have been five Spanish boys languishing
on the beaches of Barcelona. I have been a Queen sailing to a conquered empire.

Oh Chesapeake, I have grown up near your body all my life
and stopped on your shores that smell like innards of fish and birds!
You are a King my mother has never met, but only reads in the pages of my voyage.

She knows how I am tossed about in the cabin and eat salt like caviar.
The boat keeps going as though nothing else were happening—
as if she is not dying. Each hour

ripping through the bay, slicing down the innards, the belly, the rib
cage, ripping through, knot by nautical knot, in bloodstreams
and decay. My whale is fast and knows the way.

THE OTHER LIFE

Before I leave, I want to know
about the other life.

I want to hear my name
from another animal's mouth.

I want to be the tender talons
of coral or the delicacy of a crab's

underbelly. I want to be the blue fish
in the blue ocean—all current and

unhunted. I want shimmer
and fins that circle seagrass.

Would I have the same heart?
The same red muscle that pumps

too faintly to hear its own thrashing?

NOTES

The poem "The Orange Speaks" owes a debt to "The Piano Speaks" by Sandra Beasley, from her collection, *I Was the Jukebox*.

"A Room Cool as Pearls" borrows lines from Anne Carson's "New Rule" from her collection *Men in the Off Hours*.

The poem "Mother, Rest" is after "Mother, Quiet" by Martha Rhodes, from her collection, *Mother, Quiet*.

I am eternally grateful to the Washington Writers' Publishing House for selecting this collection for the Jean Feldman Poetry Prize and for believing. Thank you to the editorial board, and, especially, to Nicole Tong for her fine edits, attention, and time.

Thank you to American University and the teachers and fellow students who made me a better writer and reader. Thank you to the many instructors and students at The Fine Arts Work Center in Provincetown, MA, for the comments and workshops over the years. Also, thank you to the many teachers who have inspired and offered endless advice, specifically Elizabeth Spires, Myra Sklarew, Sidney Wade, and Cornelius Eady.

Thank you to Q for the time and support.

CPSIA information can be obtained
at www.ICGtesting.com
Printed in the USA
LVHW032310260319
611967LV00002B/355